To Claire-
For the
Moments in your
Life. Enjoy!
Kathy Brodsky

MOMENTS IN OUR LIVES - A WOMAN'S EYE VIEW...

- Kathy Brodsky

Published by Helpingwords
Manchester, NH USA

Publisher's Cataloging-in-Publication

Brodsky, Kathy.
    Moments in our lives : a woman's eyeview / Kathy Brodsky.
      p. cm.
      ISBN 0972580867

  1. Women--Poetry. 2. Family--Poetry. 3.Spiritual life--Poetry. 4. Self-actualization (Psychology)--Poetry. I. Title.

PS3602.R647M66 2004   811'.6
            QBI33-2031

The photographs contained in this book are used with the permission and under license of the photographer Cathi McGrevey; excluding photographs pages: 2, 40, 64, 94, 102.

All poems in this book were written by Kathy Brodsky.

For more information, or to order books, please contact:
Kathy Brodsky: kathy@helpingwords.com

This book is dedicated to my mother who has always been there for me. Thanks, Mom...

A Treasure Indeed!!

FOREWORD...

Three years ago, when my mother turned ninety, I wrote a poem in her honor. Until that time, I had no idea I was able to write in verse.

My poems reflect my personal experiences as a woman, and my thirty plus years as a psychotherapist. Some of the poems were developed from metaphors I created to help clients gain insights into their stressful personal situations. I used the metaphors for many years before I wrote the poems. Even though people speak of great difficulties, their stories often reveal courage, inner strength and joy.

This book of my original poems depicts a variety of pivotal events in our lives as women. The poems are a compilation of the experiences of many women, many lives woven together. In them, you may recognize moments in your own life.

However, it all started with my mother. Throughout my life she has always encouraged and supported me every step of the way... Thanks, Mom!

Kathy Brodsky, 2004

ACKNOWLEDGMENTS...

I would like to thank all the people who helped me at different stages of my poetry during these last three years.

My sons, Jeff and Greg, often traveled great distances to attend my poetry readings; their encouragement and suggestions kept me going. They have been fantastic and I can't thank them enough! Howard must definitely be mentioned, because he inadvertently helped me discover my poetic voice. Thanks for everything.

The morning swimmers at SNHU were often the first to read my poems. Their happy, positive reactions encouraged me to keep going. Thank you!

Thanks to my friends, Marilyn Cavanaugh and Karen Smith who were always there for me.

Thanks to my sister-in-law, Barbara Brodsky, who offered such clever ideas. Thanks also to Stan Brodsky, my brother-in-law, who encouraged my poetic endeavors – and a big thank you to Carroll Brodsky, who was one of the first to suggest I publish a book of my poems.

Thanks to my cousin Steve Kann who was always quick to respond with positive comments whenever I emailed a poem.

Thanks to the members of the poetry group at Barnes and Noble in Manchester, NH. They gave me my first forum to read my poems to an audience. Thanks also to Deanna who delights everyone with her warm and generous spirit at "Poetry in the Garden" each summer in Wolfeboro, NH.

Four wonderful friends have been there from the start. They have listened, cheered and always had kind words for my poems. Thank you Myrna and Mike Graf, and Gloria and Irving Fox. Your support has been fantastic!

Thank you to the Grouse Point Community, Meredith, NH, who continue to support my poems by allowing me to include them in their newsletter.

Mary Brown must be mentioned. This book wouldn't be here without Mary's wonderful book publishing class, offered by the Concord, NH Community Education Program. Mary gave us all the information we needed to publish. She is a very warm and encouraging person who told us, "You can do it!"

A huge thank you to Julia DiStefano, retired English professor at SNHU, who was my poetry editor. She kept me on track almost weekly. Julia carefully and patiently helped me edit almost all of my poems. However, sometimes I refused to make the changes she suggested. Therefore, all the remaining errors are mine.

Cathi McGrevey, is a professional photographer and a great friend who believed in my vision. She is wonderfully organized, and extremely enthusiastic. She made numerous trips to the publisher with me, dropped things off for me, and in general, Cathi kept the project moving. You will see her marvelous photographs throughout the book. Thank you so much, Cathi.

Thanks to Janet Mayberry, lifeguard at Harrogate, my mother's retirement community. Janet was always appreciative of my poems, and she was happy to display them in the pool area.

A special thank you to Helen Slocum who made a generous contribution to the publication of this book.

Thanks to my cousins Eva and Anne Sanders who allowed me to use a photo I took of them years ago.

Thank you to the fine folks at Town and Country Reprographics who put the book together. Thanks especially to Karen La Mesa, graphic designer, who designed and made the book look so good.

Thanks to my many friends – too numerous to mention individually - who listened to my poems, accepted them in emails, and responded with such positive comments.

Thank you all...

Kathy Brodsky, 2004

MOMENTS IN OUR LIVES –
A WOMAN'S EYE VIEW...

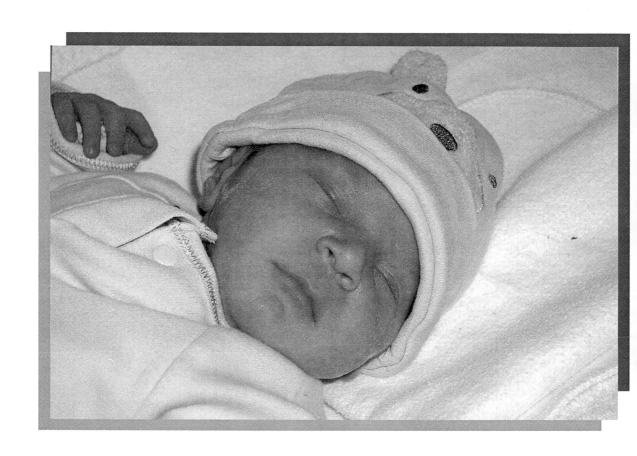

FROM A BABY'S EYE VIEW...

It's nice and warm and snug inside
I think I want to stay...
But lately things are happening -
I might not get my way...

I hear them speak and jiggle me –
A cough, a sneeze, a push –
Wonder just what's going on
Out there – but what's the rush?

At times I feel that I am stuck
So I begin to move...
I stretch my arms and kick my legs -
It's tight here in the groove...

Should I go out there, out of here
Where I'm so safe inside ?
Or do I stay, less space each day
It's time - I must decide...

Yeah, I guess I'll go for it –
Why not, I'll give a push...
I'll push and push and wiggle myself
Free from all this goosh...

Hey wait! I know all things in here-
What's out there is unknown...
I've heard them talk, they sound OK
I won't be on my own...

Now I'm pushing harder –
They seem to be helping too...
I'm almost out – But not quite yet–
I hope I don't turn blue!

I've got to get out quickly...
Look out! I'm on my way!
That person helped me with her push
I'll thank her one fine day...

Wow! Those lights are much too bright -
The air is freezing, I feel...
Going to scream so they know I'm here -
Hope they hear and know I'm real...

Good – I guess they heard me –
I'm wrapped and ready to go...
A blanket and hat for the top of my head -
I'm ready for my Big First Day Show!

WELCOME!!!

I couldn't wait to see you -
A long nine month wait, you know...

Excited, just kept watching
So thrilled having you grow...

First a heartbeat, then a flutter-
A push and then a shove...

So much movement, like the ocean-
Next a fist fight - but no gloves....

My body kept expanding-
Clothes got bigger, changed a lot

While you just kept on a growing and a going-
Thought I'd pop!!

Towards the end you started dropping-
So they told me - then I knew

That you'd soon be coming out
And we would welcome you – BRAND NEW!

Then before I knew it-
Felt you pushing out the "door"...

My entire body helped you
You exploded with a ROAR!

Thanks for coming, glad I waited-
Just so happy, that you've come...

Welcome, darling, now you're staying
We're so thrilled, you're now at home!

KIDS...

Every time they're through a phase
Another one shows up –
Burping, toilet training –
And how to use a cup...

Change goes on forever...
Definitely true...
Because it is unending
For them as well as you...

When you choose to have a baby
You're a parent all your life –
You thought when they reached 18
You'd be free of any strife...

After high school there is more...
Yes, after college too...
They come home, though on their own
No matter what you do...

Parents want to help their kids
Even more when times are rough –
Find it hard to bite their tongues
When kids arrive with stuff...

The stuff may be anything
Friends, furniture or pets–
They're looking for life's meaning
As they pay outstanding debts...

Their lives (like brought home laundry)
Need sorting, patching, mending
Looking on you see your work
As parents is unending...

Remember when you decide
To venture down baby "lane" –
You're making a lifetime commitment
Worth all of it – laughter and pain!

TERRIBLE 2's...

It was only yesterday

I held you in my arms...

Now you're running all around

Creating quite a storm...

My goodness, yes,

You're two years old

As I can plainly see...

You're separating, identifying

Your needs free from me...

I ask you if you want to-

It's "No" I get each time...

You take things – you leave them

And very often whine....

2's they say are terrible...

You're often sweet you see

When you're asleep and counting sheep

And I look in with glee!

FAMILY CHAUFFEUR...

School days I'm in my car-
From 2 'til after 6...
Pick them up / drop them off-
Really quite a trick...

After school they're scheduled...
Classes - Sports all over the place...
I crisscross the city -
It's always a frenetic pace!

My driving schedule's different
Most days of every week...
Sometimes it works smoothly
At times it's "hide and seek"...

Occasionally it happens
When no one is on time...
I wait and wait and cogitate
Sometimes I even whine...

"Please be considerate-
You know I'm in my car...
Call me if you change your plans
So I'll know where you are"...

Then I'll redo my schedule
Decide to stay or leave...
I may have to pick up others
Who are so often peeved...

The peeved ones are teenagers
Who "know" what they do
Outweighs others' needs-
Absolutely not true...

All members of our family
Should be well aware
Every person is unique-
We need to all be fair...

I figure out my schedule
With everything in mind
Yes, I'm the family chauffeur...
So glad I'm in my prime!

FIRST DAY...

Today is a big day for both of us –
Can't believe it's time for first grade!
The years have sped by much too fast –
Gathered momentum while we played...

The first day is special - we went to the store –
Bought everything brand new - so fresh...
From the top of your head to the tips of your toes
Hoped you would look great - just your best!

Yes, I admit the shopping was my little quirk –
Just wanted the day to be fine...
With video ready, I was set to begin –
Saw you wave as you stood in the line...

You stood at the bus stop with all of the kids–
Looking tiny - definitely lost...
Wanted to gather you close into my arms
And protect you – no matter the cost...

Of course I didn't – the bus soon arrived –
I watched as you slowly climbed in...
I waited and waited until you sat down
Next to someone... but hard to see then...

I decided to follow the bus with my car
All the way up to the school...
Watched through the fence and saw you arrive –
Stayed hidden to not be the fool...

My YOUNGEST! Starting SCHOOL!
No longer totally mine...
Can't protect you from all anymore –
Hope they'll do things OK down the line...

I'm walking away with large tears in my eyes –
You're a big kid, oh yes, you are...
Now that you're really in grammar school
I'll be alone again in my car!

CARS ARE SMARTER THAN WE ARE...

Cars are smarter than we are –
They stop when the tank is on "E"...
We're often stressed and continue until
We've no sense of who we should be...

Women are worst in this area
They try to be too many things...
Little by little they're slipping away
They can't see what all of this brings...

If you try to ask them a favor
They often will bite your nose...
"I'm busy," they say, "Would you please go away –
Later on I'll be washing your clothes"...

Women and men, please listen...
Time to do something for you...
A little time off – doesn't mean you're a sloth –
It will help and here's what you do...

The key to good health is balance –
In nature it works 'cause it's so...
Balance work, home and play – just do it your way –
Feel better when you learn to say, "No!"

BEST FRIEND...

A best friend is special
Because you know
You can say anything
And it never will go
Out to anyone else
Who's nearby -
Friends keep zipped lips
And always will try
To be there for each other
No matter the scene
'Cause that's what they do
They never are mean -
Best friends listen
Are not quick to judge
They're patient, supportive
And never begrudge
Our successes, or scold us
If efforts fall through
Best friends are forever...
They are tried and true!

"THE MONTHLY BILL..."

It came too early for me –
I didn't want it to come...
My mother said it would soon show up
But my body jumped the gun...

A Saturday in early fall
It showed up at my door...
I couldn't believe what I saw and felt...
Wanted to scream and roar!

I told my mother "something" was there –
I didn't know what to do...
She pulled out a pad – we had belts at the time –
Showed me how to pull through...

Mine came earlier than most girls my age
Awkward "those days" at school...
Especially in the locker room -
So embarrassed – so uncool...

Then as I got older
Luckily Tampax became the thing...
It freed me up and let me know
That I could do anything...

Now it's on – yes 28 days –
Something I know is there –
I look for it and when it shows up
I know I haven't a care!

ADOLESCENCE...

A sweet little baby
You once were I know...
Now your hormones are raging-
I'm your mother and so
I put up with arguing,
Back talk and more
Because there's a good kid
Inside of that roar...
I know as your mother
You think I'm a pain
I don't have an idea
Inside of my brain...
I know that right now
You are often unsure
And your big loud bravado
Is covering it more...
I'm your mother forever
Even if you are brash
So whenever you need me
I'll be there in a flash!

STARTING TO DRIVE...

As a mother of a 16 year old
It's a stressful time for me
She came home the other day
"I need money for my driving fee"...

I must admit the chauffeuring-thing
Is getting a little old
However the alternative
Is not so great to behold...

16 is the time
For driver education
He's so thrilled – but I'm concerned
Not feeling jubilation...

He said he signed up for
Drivers' Ed in school -
I know it's best to take it there
To learn the driving rules...

So now she needs to practice
In the family vehicle -
I really am a nervous wreck
With her behind the wheel...

I tell him to go fast or slow
And, "Watch for the thing ahead!"
I'm holding on and pressing down
As if the floor were the brake instead...

This driving stage is difficult –
Gives me too much tension
Can't wait 'til she's proficient –
Then lessened apprehension!

DATING...

Will he call now?
What's his problem?
Does he like me?
Will it work?
So many things to think of-
Is he nice or just a jerk?
What do I feel about him
When I'm with him-when I'm not...
Do we agree on basics
What of drinking, smoking, pot?
You know those things appall me-
And you know, I'm sure
If we have different values
I won't let him in my door...
What of fun and games and
Biking, hiking, swimming
Hey, you know?
Those are things I look for
With my friends so, yes, let's go!
I'll find him in the future
If he's not here yet for me...
I'll have time to use my talents
When I'm ready there he'll be!

PANTY HOSE...

Has anyone ever thought
How uncomfortable we are
With legs tied up in panty hose
So we're pretty from afar?

All women know the feeling
That panty hose is slick –
Except when there's a broken nail
So soon there is a rip...

And if we're in a hurry
To put them on too fast
They end up twisted all around
Like a tourniquet on the a _ _

Some of us have large legs
So panty hose feels like
The casing on a sausage –
It's not a pretty sight!

In case you haven't guessed it
I dislike panty hose –
If you happen to see me
I'll be wearing long-legged clothes!

WOMEN AND MEN...

When a guy breaks up with you
You think you're gonna die -
Devastating, humiliating –
You want to go and cry...

If you happen to notice
I'm looking kind of grim –
Ask me how I'm feeling –
Confused and angry with him...

Somehow you make it
'Til another catches your eye...
Maybe he'll be a perfect match–
Then in walks another guy...

Wonder who this new one is –
Sensitive and cute
Seems to be intelligent –
All the right muscles to boot...

Another guy lives nearby
He walks his dog each day –
I'd like to get to know him
But I'm shy – I pull away...

So many different men
With many different faces –
Unclear how to choose
Not even sure what basis...

Uncertain how to find my way –
But this I really know...
Girlfriends always listen –
They help us learn and grow...

Girlfriends are important –
They will see us through –
We're there for one another
Supportive when we're blue...

Guys, you're a great enhancement
You keep the species alive –
But we girls and women
Allow every one to thrive!

MY WEDDING...

Guess what! I'm getting married!
The day is almost here!
Excited! Want to tell the world
So everyone can cheer!

He asked me - I said, "Yes"-
Fantastic, romantic thing
When he knelt down on one knee
And handed me a ring...

So gorgeous, what a moment!
Something special! Can't you see?
I'm deliriously happy!
Want to shout it from the trees!

The wedding is tomorrow -
Late afternoon, you know
Celebrate with friends and family -
I'm bursting—all a glow!

Can't wait another moment!
Want the time to rush on by -
At last I have a partner...
My spouse – my special guy!!

WALKING AND RUDE MEN...

Hey, guys - Do you know how rude it is
When you walk far ahead of her?
You may want to get there right now
But her legs can't keep up with your blur...

Because as you go faster
She gets even farther away...
When you turn and look back
You see a dot instead of her face...

She definitely doesn't like it –
She may say nothing at all...
But every time you do it
She doesn't have a ball...

It makes her feel you don't care
Even though you do...
Just slow down, she'll wipe off her frown
And enjoy walking right next to you!

SUMMER HAZE...

Summer's the best time
To recharge our batteries
Because if lives stay hectic
We can't move with grace and ease...

Schedules are so crowded
In winter, spring and fall...
During those busy seasons
We try to achieve it all...

When these frenetic paces
Continue in summer as well
We don't recharge, rejuvenate
Minds and bodies go to "hell"...

Therefore, please remember
That summer is really short –
Laze around some time each day -
Healthy summer – great report!

TRANSITIONS...

Sometimes lives go smoothly -
Some bumps along the way...
Often surprised when they show up
Thought things would always stay

As they were before
When life seemed fairly easy
Now uncertain what to do -
May feel somewhat queasy...

When a new phase starts
We're plagued with mixed emotions –
Trouble moving forward –
At times feel weak and frozen...

It's good to talk to others
Close friends with caring words –
They help us express feelings -
We feel centered - less absurd...

Many universal transitions –
School, graduations and such –
Dating, marriage, babies and work –
Retirement, grandkids – what fuss...

Sometimes, we have shocks -
Difficulties unforeseen...
Separation, divorce, a child who's gay –
Sudden death – an end to a dream...

We need to know we'll make it –
At times we're all unsure –
Tomorrow is another day –
Keep moving – we'll endure!

MY CHILD'S HIGH SCHOOL GRADUATION...

Your high school graduation-
My goodness oh my gosh...
Thought this day would never come
When you had Miss McIntosh

Your 1st grade teacher-
Remember her so well...
First day of school I took you-
We listened for the bell...

That was the start of many...
Bells I mean to say
Twelve years of bells that told you
When to get up, when to stay...

So many different memories -
Activities, friends and sports...
Editing the high school paper -
"All nighter" book reports!

Don't forget the homework
Homework, homework and more...
At times it seemed to never end-
What a tremendous chore!

Now I sit here waiting
For you to march on in...
I see you walk onto the stage
With your special, wonderful grin...

Wow! They're calling your name-
I'm proud as I can be...
You did it! Yes, it's finally done
GRADUATION... Thankfully!

WHITE IN THE OREO...

Are you the white in the Oreo?
Betwixt and between old and new...
Your parents are getting older
The kids are demanding of you...

You need to get out of the middle
Take time just for you when you can...
Because if you don't – you'll be eaten alive
And no one will know where you've been...

CHILD GOING TO COLLEGE...

You're going off to college-
I really can't believe
How fast the years have come and gone-
So hard to perceive...

You can't wait to get there-
Won't be soon enough for you...
I'd like time to slow itself
So we could start anew....

Your twelve years of education-
Went by quickly for me...
I know for you they slowly passed
With extreme agony...

Now it's the end of August-
Getting ready with your stuff...
I'll help you any way I can
But it won't be enough...

Enough would mean you'd stay here
But that's not in the game
You need to leave to grow and learn-
I'll be here all the same...

Can't wait for first vacation-
Thanksgiving it will be...
You'll be back with your laundry sack-
Home again with me!!

YOU'RE BACK???

Goodness, I can't believe it-
You're now on your way back...
Thought you were set at college
Obviously not your plan of attack...

Your room is still here waiting-
Was about to change it soon
To a place for me to relax-
A little sewing room...

You know I really love you-
Want you to know it's true...
Please get your act together-
So you can start anew...

Perhaps return to college-
Take time to figure it out...
Plan to re-evaluate
Learn more of what you're about!

SLICE, CHEW, SWALLOW...

How do I start?
It all seems too much –
Like an extra large pizza -
Gigantic thick crust...

I'll take it and slice it
Make much smaller sections –
I'll cut each again
Bite and chew – no objections...

That's how I achieve things -
Slice, chew, digest...
Each challenge for me
Becomes a manageable quest!

AN ANACHRONISM...

As children we're subjected to
Our families of origin...
We're born, grow up – that's our job –
At times it's hard to grin...

We watch and learn whatever we need
To get out of there alive –
Happily, most of us do just fine –
We bring along skills to survive...

Now we're out in the big wide world
With survival skills intact...
However, there are some times
When these skills are outdated and lack

The details and information
Of what is needed right now...
Like keeping and wearing winter coats and boots
In Florida because we can't see how

To get rid of old outdated stuff –
We bring it along – just in case...
It's now an anachronism for us –
It's out of time and place!

JUST DO IT...

If you wait for joy
To show up at your door –
You'll be forever waiting -
Life will be a bore...

Nothing's gonna happen
If you sit and take no action –
You'll be tired, little fun –
Not much satisfaction...

Move and leave that chair
Get yourself all dressed –
The sooner that you do it
You'll begin to feel your best...

You need to leave the comfort
Of your home and go outside...
What you may discover
Is a sense of self and pride!

THE TIME THING...

Sometimes if I'm a little late
It's fine, I really feel...
Easier on my body
Less commotion, brakes don't squeal...

Lots of people that I know
Are really time obsessed -
When others arrive a little late
They have no time for jest...

Compulsive punctuality
Stresses me, I hate to say
Because I tend to rush around...
Arrive almost breathless that day...

For certain kinds of appointments -
Doctor, dentist or hair...
I always try to be on time
Then wait patiently in my chair...

But for casual get-togethers
I'd rather a give and take...
So happy when people are more like me –
Much relieved, there's less at stake!

STRESS...

Used to think life was fine-
Took things day by day...
Now I am so overwrought-
Can't get out of my own way...

Many different issues-
Difficult to begin...
If I list the problems
I'll have a chance to win...

Let's first look at home life-
Used to feel fine, happy here...
Lately I'm disgruntled-
Now need a supportive ear...

I take it out on family
Who aren't the cause or blame...
But they are nearest to me-
Hate to give them such pain...

I really want to be kinder
To everyone close to me
Because holding onto my anger
Keeps me distant constantly...

At work there's always chaos-
Changing rearranging the place...
One day I have a certain boss
Next day a whole different face...

Certainly hard to get used to-
This company changes a lot...
Much talk of downsizing-
Don't know if my job will be dropped...

Too much stress on me daily
Have to take charge of my life...
Take time for meditation
To quiet all of this strife...

I'll reassess my values-
Should have done it long ago...
Retain what's important-
Let anger and pressures go...

Begin a list of options-
Consider possibilities...
Focus more on positive thoughts-
Happy again to be me!

A LONGER DAY...

A longer day, I'm thinking –
A longer day, yes sir...
It would be for anyone –
No matter who – him or her...

The idea is really simple –
It would work according to need -
Request a few more hours whenever
We need less stress, more ease...

Just imagine getting
An extended day at times...
Longer to complete a project
Or hear a nursery rhyme...

What a fantastic option!
More hours in the day!
How would we gain access?
Press a button or say, "Hey"...

Who would give acceptance?
Would we sometimes be denied?
It might be complicated –
How should we all decide?

How would it be with others
Whose day is still the same?
Do we reconcile the time
Or play a waiting game?

For now it's 24 hours –
It is the usual thing...
But it's certainly fun to think
What a l-o-n-g-e-r day would bring!

REPOSE...

Once in a while
It is a treat
Before sitting upright
With dangling feet

To stay in bed
With eyes still closed
Doze on and off
Remain reposed...

Do not a thing
Nothing at all –
Just lie relaxed
Chest rise and fall

Until the need
To up and dangle
Feet beneath
Brain must untangle...

Brand new day
Is now to start
Must up and go
And do my part!

TOASTY, COZY...

When we're toasty, cozy -
We feel so safe and warm
With a fine sense overall
Nothing can do us harm...

Outside our homes in winter
It's freezing and it's wet –
Gathered with our loved ones
'Round the fire - just the best!

Sometimes in the summer
After a long swim
We're tired, cold and hungry
Hot chocolate makes us grin...

If late at night exhausted
We tumble into bed
Toasty, cozy is the feeling
Pulling covers up to head...

Enveloped in a warm bath
Sometimes bubbles, sometimes not –
Troubles seem to melt away -
Hot tubs just hit the spot!

Some folks enjoy the comfort
Of coffee or of tea
Sit and drink a full hot cup –
The world seems right, you see...

Remember cozy feelings
Of a parent and a child
At bedtime sharing story time -
The memory makes us smile...

Simply the most precious
Toasty, cozy feeling we know -
Big bear hugs from those we love -
The very best warm glow!

BAKING...

The smells and tastes of baking
Remind me of long ago
Sitting, helping in mom's kitchen –
A noisy, lively show...

The kitchen was the center
For everyone nearby –
Tempting aromas, feasts for all––
Mom's cookies, cakes and pies...

Vanilla, cinnamon – delicious
Great scents I still treasure
Butter and flour mixed by hand
So much 'squooshy' pleasure!

I remember feeling lucky
When the bowl was given to me...
I held the big mixing spoon -
Scraped and licked both...IMMACULATELY!

"Do other bowls need cleaning?
I'm waiting, can't you see ?
Ready, willing, happy and able
To lick them for you for free!"

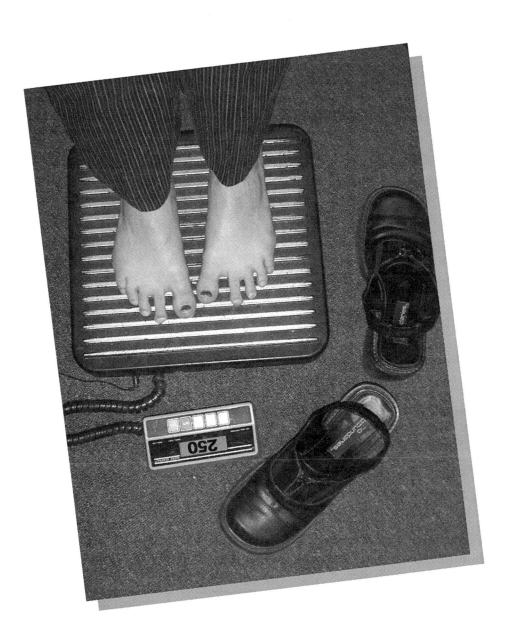

WEIGHT GAIN...

These pants used to fit -
Now they're a little tight...
It's as if I gained weight
While sleeping last night...

The weight crept up so slowly...
It sneaked up from the rear...
Either these pants shrunk in the wash
Or my thighs have gained inches - oh dear!

Not sure what I should do
About this recent event
Because all the pants in my closet
Fit me when I was content...

I was content with my body
But with this change in size...
Stomach, thighs and rear have grown...
No longer the image I prize...

Now I need to make choices
About how I eat and move...
Maybe I'll join a health club-
Get my body back into the groove...

Start moving as I used to
When things felt right, you see...
Need to rethink my food intake...
Celebrate a new improved me!

LOSS / GAIN...

When something awful happens
Life looks dismal / Nothing's right...
But somehow we rally –
Get through the arduous plight...

While we do the tumble -
Down and up – around
We're using all our energy
To keep both feet on the ground...

Later on we notice
That through the painful time
We've gained something along the way –
Knowledge / Strength combined...

ORGANIZED...

I wish I were organized
With everything in place...
I have trouble doing it
I pile, have little space...

Clutter is a problem –
Tidy – no, I'm not...
Wish I did things differently –
"Have you seen my other sock?"

Guess I am a "piler" –
A person who makes piles...
If they were giving credit -
"Piles" grade would make me smile...

I'd get an A+ easily
Because I make them well...
Piles are many - often high-
Grow higher, then they swell...

When I have to find
Something I'm looking for
I have to see which pile it's in
Before going out the door...

This takes time, of course it does –
You can guess the rest...
Now I'm later than I want –
"Pile searching" is a quest!

I have some friends who are the type
With everything in place...
Their kitchen counters sparkle
Because nothing's in their space...

They're also ones whose tables gleam
Whenever there is light because
there's nothing on the top
To keep it out of sight...

In my house on the other hand
Wherever there is room
It means I have a place to put
Quite anything I assume...

The two that are the hardest
Are the paper things and clothes...
They pile and clutter easily-
This stuff just grows and grows...

I want to be the other way –
I want my house to gleam...
Be able to have people come
No three-month notice to clean...

I've bought the books to organize –
I do it, then it's undone...
Guess I'll have to resign myself
I'm not one of the tidier ones!

IT'S UP TO US...

We must live our lives
However they are...
Though others criticize
Judging us from afar...

Completely alone
As we walk in our shoes...
Always consequences
Whatever we choose...

Sometimes we're off -
We miss the center dot-
Hope to get a second chance
To take another shot...

Be ready to try again...
Little is cast in stone
Until the very end
When nothing's left but bones...

I THOUGHT I WAS SET...

Always thought that I was set -
Got married years ago...
But things have changed and life is not
As then, when life was slow...

Slow at first, but then sped up
When the family started to grow...
First child born – another came –
Again I began to show...

Couldn't believe I was pregnant again –
After three, I'd had enough...
Morning sickness, gaining weight -
Had my tubes tied - it was rough...

All the kids got older...
We grew older, as well...
My spouse and I slowly drifted apart –
Then came the notice from hell...

It said the thing I dreaded most –
The words hit home and then
"irreconcilable differences"...
Divorce was around the bend...

Now I'm trying to heal and mend –
It's certainly hard to do...
I'm gonna do it – I know I can
I'm building my life anew!

THE EX-ES...

Dealing with the ex-es –
Of mine and then of his...
Stressful each and every way –
No never ending bliss...

If only ex-es were willing
To pay attention to reason –
We'd do better for the kids
In each and every season...

Days are set for back and forth
And overnights, we know –
Then comes a call – they want a change –
A never-ending show...

Holidays are such a strain
Though written in the order –
"I want more time" – "No take them now"...
Lots of change - disorder...

Money issues cause distress –
Kids caught in the middle –
"Where's the check?" – "It's in the mail" –
"I paid for that" – "Too little"...

Somehow we all make it through –
At times we wonder how...
Life goes on for them, for us –
Kids grow - less ex-strain now!

WAVES...

First I didn't understand-
Was numb all of the time...
Then the crying started –
Couldn't stop - just felt like dyin'...

Fear then came and I was scared –
Anger followed suit...
Suddenly felt so all alone
Thought life should get the boot...

This went on in ups and downs
Then downs and ups again...
The roller coaster I was on
Never had an end...

Slowly then the dips were less
The ride seemed much more even...
Noticed then some rays of sun
Yes, thought I must be dreamin'

Sun grew brighter, stayed out more,
The gloom was less profound...
Still at times the waves erupt
And pound me to the ground...

Like the ocean with the waves -
When they come I duck...
At times I'm looking elsewhere,
Get sucked in with all the muck...

A wave can be most anything
That reminds me of it all...
A song, a smell, a face, a noise –
Might not know the exact recall...

Suddenly back to the time or place
It's all just so "right there"...
Need to allow myself to breathe –
Stretch or get out of my chair...

Pick up the phone to call a friend
Or wipe my tears away...
Waves may show up once in a while –
Don't want them here every day...

I've talked to others who understand
They say that time will heal...
That day can't come too soon for me
Get unstuck, move forward and feel...

Today I am more stable
Than I was some time ago –
Starting to feel more like myself –
Happier, ready to grow...
Now, if a wave or two
Comes to knock me around...
I'll see it coming from far away...
I'm on more solid ground!

GIVE A LITTLE...

Every story is different –
Each one quite unique...
According to our origin
Hope to land on our two feet...

When we look at something
We see it through our eyes –
Assume the way we see it
Is right because we're wise...

Often there are others
Who see things differently –
We need to see their viewpoint
Which to them is right, you see...

When we fail to do that
We fumble deed and word –
Tenacious in our thinking -
All lose which is absurd...

Viewpoints may be different
As long as we can give
A little from each corner
In the "middle" we can "live"!

SON'S WEDDING...

Our son is getting married-
He says she's the one for him...

Hope she appreciates all his traits
Down to his wonderful grin...

He has always been so special-
Cute in every way....

Smart and strong and sensitive-
Even when he played

He had a sense of fairness
Considerate, honest, kind...

Always there for others-
Best friend you'd ever find...

I hope that I can do it-
My son is now all grown...

I want to welcome her as kin
When I see her in her gown...

He'd only pick a winner –
Of that I know I'm right...

His new bride will be great for him –
I'll welcome her tonight!

DAUGHTER'S WEDDING...

Wow! My daughter's getting married-
I'm the mother of the bride...

It seems as if just yesterday
I held her deep inside...

Very, many feelings-
So happy, then so sad

Our little girl becomes a wife
I know we should be glad...

Her dad and I are happy-
Excited, yes, we are...

Ready with a welcome for
Our brand new son-in-law...

We have seen him with our daughter-
We know he'll treat her right...

All couples have their ups and downs-
Even when they fight

We hope they'll kiss and make up-
Correct things that go wrong...

Today their lives become entwined...
I hear the wedding song...

CONNECTIONS...

When we're connected
To a person, place or thing –
It's a special feeling
The connection really brings...

Connection is a linking
From one being to another...
Often very powerful
Like a baby to its mother...

Joyful memories connect us
To a place we've been before –
Special folks we met there
Gave us so much more...

Six degrees of separation –
Something we can test...
We're told a mere six people
Separate us from the rest...

Most important connections –
Others will agree -
Links of tears and laughter
Shared with friends and family!

MY GUT...

There's a place inside of me –
I call it "my gut"...
A special spot where I have stored
Feelings – a sense of stuff...

It senses what is right for me –
Also what is wrong...
It's there to keep myself intact -
Helps me get along...

My gut may say, "Yes, go for it " –
Or "Stop! There's danger ahead"...
If I don't listen I may regret
What I did or what I said...

This gut, my intuition
Has been there from the start...
It often knows much better than I –
Should I leave, stay, do my part...

So when that "oh, oh" feeling
Comes a knocking at my door...
I know if I pay attention
I'll be much happier with the score!

BREATH...

Breathing's not an option –
We do it or we die...
Whenever we're scared witless
We hold our breath – but why?

We've heard others say it...
"So afraid I thought I'd die"-
Better to take a deep breath
Let go with an audible sigh...

That's what they do in yoga –
Breath is a large focus there...
Wherever there are tight muscles
Deep breathing allows them some air...

At times breath helps us balance –
A moment of insight and peace...
Time can make all the difference
In relationships – also in speech...

Take a moment to breathe...
Deeply, slowly and then
You'll feel more relaxed and centered...
Able to function again!

COLD BREEZES...

Whenever I am somewhere
And someone starts to sneeze...
My mind screams, "Full alert, move quickly away" –
Because I know in a breeze

Of really less than a second
Their germs will start to come...
Then a cold will consume me
With sore throat and nose on the run...

This is a major problem
For me, I have to say
Because in the type of job I do
I travel lots everyday...

In meetings it happens often
I turn the other way...
If I know the person, I may ask,
"Do you have a cold today?"

When traveling I'm subjected
To whomever sits next to me...
At the first sign of a sneeze or cough
I change seats suddenly...

Summer's not as difficult
Because fewer germs are around...
In winter those with sneezes and coughs
All show up wherever I'm found...

They call me a hypochondriac –
Which is certainly fine by me...
As long as those with cold sniffles, flu germs
Avoid my proximity!

TAKING CARE OF PARENTS...

The kids are finally grown and out...
"Ah – freedom once again..."
But now my aging parents
Need my constant attention...

I feared the day would never come
When kids would leave the nest...
They did but now my time is spent
With parents who protest...

They need assistance in many ways -
I drive them to doctors and stores
Give housing advice, help pay their bills-
Roles changed - now even score...

I think of how my life is
And how I thought it would be...
Always assumed when the kids left
I could concentrate on me...

What I didn't realize-
And what I know today
Is - as long as I have my parents
They'll be part of my every day!

SIMPLIFY...

The trend is now to simplify
Our homes and our lives too
Except it is extremely hard...
Always things to do...

I was told to make a list
I'm very good at that –
Unfortunately the list just grows -
Keeps on getting fat...

Making lists is not enough
To clear my cluttered place -
I better start to throw things out
Or else I'll lose the race...

Have to make some changes –
Get past this gloomy room...
Want to run and dance and play -
Plan to move stuff very soon...

Joy and freedom almost here –
Gaining momentum as I go...
Making space for my new life...
I feel the fresh energy flow!!

MID LIFE...

I'm a woman at mid-life
Whose kids are grown

Finally there's time
For a life of my own...

What's hard I discover
While jump-starting my plan

Is the difficulty I have
Wondering just who I am...

Numerous pathways
From which to choose -

Unsure - unclear
Where to start - what to lose...

Get more education?
Go off on my own?

Will it cost much ?
Do I need a loan?

Follow my partner's footsteps?
What would that do?

Go in my own direction?
I haven't a clue...

So many options -
How will I know?

Don't have all the answers -
I'll get up and go...

I'll take a new highway
To places unknown...

As long as it's my way
I'll always be home!

OUR QUEST...

Each of us is on a quest
Searching all the time –
Frequent stops to lay our heads
Think this will be sublime...

Often find as years go by
That we and they have changed...
Look and wait to see what's next -
Sometimes we rearrange...

Then begin to seek new ways
Some different than before -
No need to throw all that came
Before this current door...

Remember we are all a part
Of now and what was then...
Take the best but save the rest
We may want it once again!

LITTLE BY LITTLE....

Little by little we do things –
Little by little they're done...
Few things happen spontaneously –
Once in a while a home run...

One foot in front of the other
Gets us from place to place...
Speed isn't the main objective -
More important to finish the race...

To finish we need a beginning –
To begin we need a goal...
A goal is our destination
To strive for – body and soul...

 Goal or destination
Maybe fancy at times mundane...
However we approach it –
The objective is where we should aim...

Rearranging a closet
A daunting task to see...
Clear out all the old stuff –
Put the rest back properly...

Destinations can be easy –
Like driving to the store...
But we don't get into the car
'til we know what we're driving for...

Achievement may seem impossible
With family, job, home or school...
When stuck we remind ourselves
To remember the simple rule...

Little by little we do things –
Little by little they're done...
Few things happen spontaneously -
Once in a while a home run!

TAKING CHARGE...

When we don't take charge
We let others do it for us –
We're in the backseat of a car -
Someone else is driving our stuff...

We need to get into the front –
Tell the driver, "It's time to leave" –
Now it's all up to us...
Where we go, how we live, what we achieve...

AROUND MENOPAUSE...

A bright hot face I'm feeling
Then a burning, then a sweat -

They say I'm not in menopause-
I know I'm close and yet

I'm having trouble with my body
Feeling "antsy" out of sorts

Moods are swinging up and down-
I need a full report...

Lots of trouble sleeping-
Wake up burning, soaking wet...

Need to throw the covers off me-
Then back on – I'm just a mess...

Should discuss this with my doctor
So I can start to plan...

Manage with exercise and diet?
Question a hormone regimen?

Want to stop this feeling-
Get past it – move along...

Friends who've gotten through it
Are singing a brand new song!

LINES IN FACE AND WISDOM...

When I was much younger
I saw pimples all the time –
Now looking in the mirror
I see lots of experience lines...

No idea where they came from –
Wish they'd disappear
They're here now and won't go away -
Worse – more appear each year...

I look around at others
Similar to my age...
I wonder if they notice
The extra lines on my face...

The other day it was awful –
Something else occurred...
Where my skin used to be firm
My chin has an extra curve...

Not exactly double –
Definitely not as tight –
I know I'll never see twenty again
Even wishing with all my might...

I now have years of experience...
Which I'm sure is really OK –
My face has the lines to prove it
As I grow with each passing day!

TO BE OR NOT TO BE GRAY...

As the years creep up on us
Our hair is not the same...
What was always rich in color
Has gray added to our mane...

First we notice one hair
Looks different from the rest –
We locate it and pull it out –
Our hair now looks its best...

We do this locate-pull thing
For a while, but as we do
The gray spreads even wider –
How to approach this slew?

Such a big decision –
We all must make, it seems...
Just let nature take its course
Or should we intervene?

If gray overtakes us
We hope that it will be
A rich full head of steel and white
On top for all to see...

Always can reach for a bottle –
At hairdresser or at home
To get rid of interlopers
Who've invaded our rich-colored dome...

To be or not to be gray -
A question we all face...
No matter who, it matters not –
We hope to age with grace!

HISTORICAL PERSPECTIVE...

At times I'm upset with me
About something I did or said -
Though it may have been long ago
The thoughts replay in my head...

What was I doing, thinking then?
Why did I act that way?
How did I let another choose
For me that long-ago day?

I'm here now and looking back
From a wiser point of view...
We gain our wisdom over time
From everything we do!

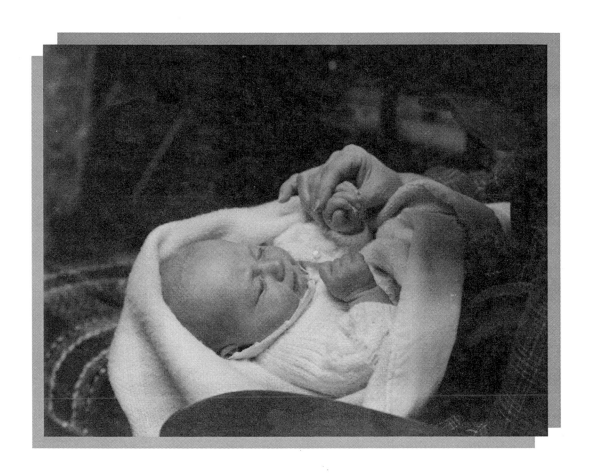

GRANDCHILD'S COMING...

Guess what—they said a BABY!
Can't believe that's what I heard...

I listened so intently...
I hardly said a word!

Wow! I'm happy and excited!
They did it, so they did!

We're gonna have a baby!
We can use the family crib...

I'll see if I can find it –
Up in the attic, I think...

It may need some redoing -
A new mattress - blue or pink?

We're deliriously happy
The baby's coming, on its way...

Don't think that I can stand it
Can hardly wait 'til the birth day!

GRANDPARENT...

Being a grandparent
Is a special joy –
Whether it's a pretty girl
Or handsome little boy...

Love to be there with them –
Make plans in a huddle –
When their parents go away
Lots of time to cuddle...

Whenever we do anything
No matter what we choose –
Lots of fun in every way –
Together we can't lose!!

MY DOG...

Eagerly waits when I come home
Each day of every week...
Wants to be right next to me –
Loves to play hide and seek...

Constant, loving companion –
Listens closely to everything...
Interprets what I'm thinking
Without my saying a thing...

Happy when we're together –
Sad when we're apart...
Hates when I prepare for work –
Knows I'll be leaving her out...

Happiest times are weekends –
Together each night and day...
Lots of time to snuggle –
Really have time to play...

Most fun is the car window
When open it's really a blast...
Head leaning out as far as can be
Staring at cars as we pass...

This one's quite a loud breather -
Smooshed up nose as it is...
Comforting, hearing noises so sweet
Next to me as I sit - reminisce...

When she goes where she shouldn't –
The couch, recliner or bed...
She's so special in every way
I can't stay mad - so instead

I hold her, love her and tell her
How very much she means to me...
She's my doggy forever –
At least I wish she could be!

RETIREMENT...

It can start at any age
Used to be 65
Now some do it younger
Some folks wait 'til 85...

Whenever it is, it's all the same
Yet very different too...
Whatever age you switch gears
A new phase starts for you...

For some, it means one job is done
Another is in the wings –
For others, it's the start
Of golf and various things...

Many people leave, go south –
Call themselves "snowbirds"...
When north cold winds begin to blow
They flee, go south in herds...

In warmer spots – relax, swim a lot
Sun and shade all day...
Won't return until warm spring days
Replace winter's barren decay...

Some retirees
Stay - don't move away
Spend time with friends and family-
Work or play each day...

Schedule their days quite casually –
No hectic rushing for them
Now have time to try new things -
May return to school again...

Who or where, all say the same,
"Can't imagine just how
I worked a job – a full-time one –
Wouldn't go back to that now!"

WE LEARN AS WE GO...

Many, many years ago
When we were very small
We thought we knew just everything -
KNEW we knew it all...

As long as we had answers
For parents, school or friends -
We were focused – had the facts
Knew how to achieve our ends...

Now, black and white are blending
As years have come and gone –
More gray – much less certainty
In sorting right from wrong...

We're wiser and more tolerant -
Can't know everything–
We're learning more acceptance
To cope with what life brings!

LOSING A SPOUSE / PARTNER...

He was always next to me
Where I went, he'd be...

But he's no longer there...
I look over at his chair

Which is empty now, you know-
He was the first to go...

Went through life side by side-
Loved going for a ride...

We had the normal ups and downs-
He had a silly little frown...

Miss him every single day-
Wish he'd be here and stay...

If we had just one more day
I'd hug him, then I'd say

"Even though my life goes on-
It's not the same now that you're gone..."

THE PEOPLE IN OUR LIVES...

We want the people in our lives
To be around forever
But nature interferes with this –
A little like the weather...

Often there are storms ahead –
We know of them in advance -
At other times they just show up
Unexpected, big change in plans...

In our lives, too, we often know
When someone is very ill
Sooner or later we will find out
They are eternally still...

Sometimes people are seemingly fine –
And everything is OK...
Then we hear they suddenly died –
No advance notice today...

No matter how it happens –
We're never really prepared...
We want life to go on for those
Whose lives we have always shared...

OLD AGE...

I'm getting older-
What felt fine is now an ache...

Used to do things easily-
Now I need a break...

Take time to do things slowly-
More time to do things right

Or I could fall and break a bone
A scary, horrible fright...

Once so many people
I knew a time ago...

Quite a few no longer here
It was their time to go...

So hard now for me often
But I refuse to stop...

My life will keep on moving
Until the very last drop!

FOREVER...

Nothing's forever...
We want it to be –
The newness of love
The buds on a tree...
Think things will stay
As they once were...
In houses or jobs
Situations occur
As times change
Events take their toll
People come and they go
For everyone...All...
Buildings that once were
No longer are there –
When we go back
Only memories to share...
Forever is not...
But that's really OK –
Enjoy what is now -
Be present each day!

BRAND NEW FRESH...

Every day when I awake
A unique opportunity dawns –
Brand new fresh start lies ahead
For me to see what spawns...

I can choose to do things
I've always done before...
But if I change direction
I may find a different door...

I should be mindful of my mood -
Emotions are a factor –
Happy or sad – anxious or not –
Much depends upon laughter...

Brand new fresh day welcomes us!
Blank slate for everyone...
How we use it - what we say -
Our own individual creation!

"Never too late"
believe in the Results!
Claire Knowles!

POEMS...

AFTERWORD...

Thank you for choosing this book. I hope you enjoyed reading my poems as much as I enjoyed writing them.

I would love to hear from you - your responses to a particular poem - or to the book in general. If you have suggestions for other poems for another book, I would like to know those as well. Please contact me at:

helpingwords.com
Custom and life-event poems, cards, mugs, message magnets

When you have an occasion
You want to write something for
I can do it for you in a rhyming way
So it's not your time or your chore...

It may be work-related
A leisure-time event
A family celebration
Anytime you want words sent...

Tell me the event and info –
If you want it serious or light...
A chance I can do it quickly for you –
Within days or later that night...

It's fun to get out a message –
Give people a personal note...
email kathy@helpingwords.com
Delighted to help with your quote...

Again thanks,
Kathy Brodsky, 2004

Thanks to my special girl who assisted with every part of this book!